PRAISE FOR

THE SOUL FEELS ITS WORTH

"Hillery Schanck has written a wonderful accompaniment to a masterpiece of music. I highly recommend that you take the time to listen, read and reflect; you won't come out the other side the same."

—**Wm Paul Young**, Author of *The Shack, Cross Roads, Eve* and *Lies We Believe About God*

"Mystics have always insisted that a real encounter with God is an ineffable experience. Words simply can't express it. There is, however, music. The heavenly messenger who first heralded the Incarnation was accompanied by an angelic choir. Where words leave off, music picks up and completes the task. Plato said, 'Music gives a soul to the universe, wings to the mind, flight to the imagination and life to everything.' Handel's *Messiah* is a transcendent voice that has nurtured the world in that way for nearly three centuries. Now Hillery Schanck and Daniel Boothe have joined arms with the *Messiah* in a partnership that will enrich your Advent season in a transformative manner. Take your time with these meditations in *The Soul Feels Its Worth*. Open your heart and watch the music and meditations bring Life as the ancient declaration of the gospel enlightens your mind, elevates your emotions and energizes the Advent season in a way that is nothing less than mystical."

—**Dr. Steve McVey**, Best-selling author of *Grace Walk*

"What you are holding is a multi-sensory invitation into the very heart of God. Hillery stands before you, grinning, and rocking back and forth, nearly shaking, like a kid at Christmas. He is holding the words, composition and music to Handel's Messiah. In all of his careful study, reflection, and thoughtful invitation, you are offered an astonishing gift. Take your time with this. *The Soul Feels Its Worth* is not to be just read, but absorbed. He guides you into God's love. He guides you into the history and story. He guides you into your own story. You finish feeling not ashamed, but instead free in your faith, alive and filled with innocent joy, knowing your full worth, as one indwelled with God Himself."

—**John Lynch**, Co-author of *The Cure,* and author of
On My Worst Day

"*The Soul Feels Its Worth* is a new but rooted kind of Advent journey. Hillery gives heed to the intellect and to our emotions as well, engaging the imagination and most importantly the heart. It's beautiful."

—**Ron Block**, Alison Krauss & Union Station

"I was first drawn to *The Soul Feels Its Worth* by its intriguing cover, then by the noble intention of the project, and finally by the inviting words Hillery Schanck has so well crafted. It is hard for all of us to slow down in our everyday lives and appreciate the gifts God has so generously given us. It is especially hard during the hectic days leading up to Christmas, when we should take time to appreciate his most precious gift—the gift of his dearly beloved son. If you struggle with that during the Christmas holidays, this book will help. What I love about it is the emphasis on 'feeling the story of God.' The scriptural lyrics of Handel's *Messiah*, along with its stirring music, help usher those feelings into the presence of God, reaching a crescendo in a personal encounter with him in prayer."

—**Ken Gire**, Author of *Moments with the Savior* and
Windowsof the Soul

"Every lyric in Handel's *Messiah* is Scripture; each word carries the power to change and renew. But as Hillery Schanck observes (and as Handel no doubt intended), the music is what equips us to feel transformation. In breaking this masterpiece down into 25 lyric- and music-based daily devotions, Hillery invites us to step into the story and experience the full scope of Advent—not just with our eyes or our ears, but in the very depths of our soul."

—**Jodie Berndt**, Best-selling author of the Praying the Scriptures book series

"I wasn't prepared for what I would experience when a good friend asked me to review *The Soul Feels Its Worth*. A classically trained musician who departed that space a few decades ago for the technology-driven pop music world, I expected a standard book that dryly referenced music from my former life. Who would have thought a QR Code, Spotify playlist, coupled with Scripture and insightful devotionals could turbo charge Handel's masterpiece and produce a longing for a deeper relationship with Jesus the Messiah? Wow! It's on my Advent calendar for this year and hope it will be on yours as well.

—**Allen Weed**, Founder & CEO, interlinc

"The message of this devotional book was summed up by this wonderful statement made by the author. 'After binding the strong one and redeeming human nature from the grave, Jesus carries it all to the throne of God. The gifts Jesus then received from His Heavenly Father, gifts of the spirit, He now passes on to us to build up the new temple of the living God . . . you and me . . . the permanent place. "I will be [your] God, and [you] shall be My people."' "

—**Craig Snyder**, Executive Director Grace Walk Miniseries

"Music is such a rich and significant resource to our devotional life. When used appropriately it has the power to unlock the hidden places of our heart in a way that no other medium can. Combined as it does here with daily words of encouragement and exhortation this ground breaking and original take on Handel's *Messiah* will stir and strengthen your understanding of the magnitude and magnificence of the God of all Grace."

—**Dave Bilbrough**, Songwriter and worship leader

"Handel's *Messiah* is the story of Jesus Christ set to music, and Hillery Schanck uses this powerful composition to give us access to God's heart. Through a 25-day devotional, one that can be used privately or in a group, Schanck reveals how the love of God can be felt in both Scripture and music, not only touching hearts but transforming minds. Your soul will be nourished by this journey with *Messiah*."

—**Henry G. Brinton**, Presbyterian pastor and author of the novel *City of Peace*

"Hillery R. Schanck has produced a truly unusual book of Advent devotions based on the words of Handel's famous *Messiah*. Each day's devotion includes a section of Handel's libretto, questions designed to guide the reader, and—most remarkably—a special recording of a performance. The combination is dynamic."

—**Dean Robertson**, Author of *Looking for Lydia, Looking for God*

The Soul Feels It's Worth:

*An Advent Devotional Through the Music and
Scriptures of Handel's Messiah*

by Hillery R. Schanck

ISBN 978-1-63393-788-8

Published by

 köehlerbooks™

210 60th Street
Virginia Beach, VA 23451
800-435-4811
www.koehlerbooks.com

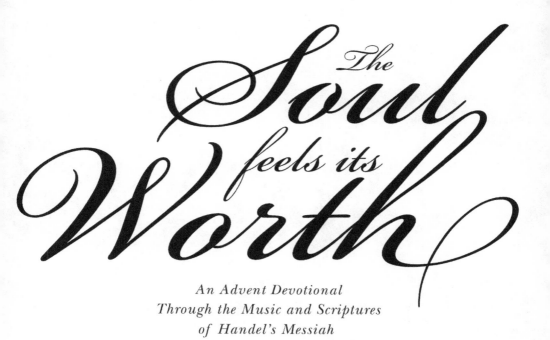

The Soul feels its Worth

An Advent Devotional
Through the Music and Scriptures
of Handel's Messiah

INCLUDES ONLINE ACCESS TO A FULL
RECORDING BY SYMPHONICITY DIRECTED
BY DANIEL W. BOOTHE

HILLERY R. SCHANCK

VIRGINIA BEACH
CAPE CHARLES

AUTHOR'S NOTE

TABLE OF CONTENTS

FOREWORD

*I*t is probably safe to say that Handel's *Messiah* has been heard by more people than any other piece of classical music. *Messiah* is an oratorio, a kind of dramatic devotional entertainment that in Handel's time was usually performed during Lent as a substitute for opera. Now it is usually performed, broadcast, or listened to at home during Advent, so the book you have before you was written to facilitate using it for meditative devotions during Advent in preparation for the celebration of Christmas.

Does listening to *Messiah* and meditating upon it during Advent violate Handel's expectation that it would be performed during Lent? Or more to the point, is its message somehow skewed if we focus on it at the "wrong" time of year? Certainly not. In Handel's time, oratorios were usually performed during Lent because secular entertainments like opera were considered inappropriate during that time of year. So oratorios, with their sacred subjects, typically from the Old Testament, took the place of operas during Lent.

Apart from the customs of the time, the specific content of *Messiah* is appropriate at any time. It tells the whole story of salvation—Jesus' birth, ministry, suffering, death, resurrection, and ascension and the spread of the Gospel—and culminates in celebrating his Second Coming and eternal reign. *Messiah* is an oratorio for all seasons. But personally, I find it particularly fitting during Advent, the beginning of a new liturgical year. This is partly because it has become customary;

but I also like it during Advent because the beginning of the liturgical year is a good time to hear and devotionally contemplate the whole story that will unfold again during the coming year.

So how is one to listen to *Messiah*? At the risk of sounding overly simple, I would say that the first thing a new listener needs to know is something that a veteran listener needs to be reminded of—namely, that *Messiah* is a story. It is not a liturgy and it is not theology. It is something more primal; it is the story that is the foundation for all Christian worship and the grist for all Christianity's theological mills. On reading Dante's *Divine Comedy* for the first time, a friend of the writer Dorothy Sayers, said, "It isn't at all what I expected. It's like someone sitting there in an arm-chair and telling you a story." *Messiah* is something like that too. Handel's manner may be too grand and solemn to imagine him telling the story from an armchair. Nevertheless, telling "the old, old story" is what *Messiah* is all about.

Handel was a master storyteller. He had to be because through much of his career his main occupation was composing opera. He was an opera composer without peer. He was unsurpassed in taking the stories of ancient heroes, the subject matter of most Baroque operas, and setting them to music that vividly and movingly portrayed the emotions engendered by the events of the story. So as an experienced opera composer, and one without peer, he had all the musical skills he needed when he turned to oratorio. In oratorio, he found hero stories that were more than suitable replacements for the hero stories of opera. Instead of telling the stories of, say, Julius Caesar or Richard the Lionhearted, he applied his considerable musical storytelling abilities to the stories of the great Old Testament heroes like Joshua and Esther. *Messiah* also tells the story of a hero—but an infinitely greater hero. Its hero is the Shepherd who feeds his flock, the Lamb who was slain and redeemed us by his blood, the risen and ascended King of kings and Lord of lords who now reigns eternally.

CALVIN R. STAPERT
Professor of Music Emeritus, Calvin College
Author, *Handel's Messiah: Comfort for God's People*

FROM THE

With a desire to understand God better, I have spent innumerable hours studying Scripture and reading religious texts attempting to uncover deeper truths about Him. But in all that effort, I find that I sometimes miss the fact that He simply wants to be in a relationship with me. That is because I am reading the Bible like a manual, not like a powerful story with accounts of real people dealing with conflict and emotion, tragedy and hope . . . just like we all do.

Charles Jennens crafted an abridged story of the Messiah using only Scripture. He gave this *libretto* to Handel, and Handel brilliantly composed music that reanimated the words to reflect the intended emotions. Using musical elements like *vibrato* and *prestissimo*, he makes the story of the Messiah come alive again to us and we experience something different, something necessary about God's Word—His heart.

The apostle Paul's prayer over the Ephesians becomes his prayer for us: *That you may . . . know the love of Christ which surpasses knowledge, that you may be filled up to all the fullness of God.* My hope is that through this devotion—combined with reading and listening, meditating and praying—you will experience the love of God, through the story of His Messiah, and it will reconnect you back to Him in a vibrant, meaningful relationship.

This devotional guide walks you through a twenty-five-day adventure of the story of our Messiah, with the purpose of helping you know and feel the love of Christ. This story was intended for you.

FROM THE *Maestro*

hen I arrived as the new music director and conductor for Symphonicity, I was most drawn to the group's genuine community-centric mission. This was best displayed in my first *Messiah* Sing-Along performance with Symphonicity at the Sandler Center for the Performing Arts in December 2017. Over 1,300 people attended that performance, and nearly as many of them sang loudly and proudly with each of the choruses. With tears in my eyes, I realized I had never seen or heard anything quite like that in my entire career.

Author Hillery R. Schanck and publisher John Koehler attended that performance and were inspired as well. Schanck already had an idea for a devotional text that would help reveal the meaning and beauty of the masterpiece by George Frideric Handel. But they needed a partner to complete their vision and provide an original recording. They contacted Symphonicity to discuss how our iconic *Messiah* tradition of nearly forty years might be the perfect match. We all immediately agreed that it seemed like divine intervention.

I believe Symphonicity is one of the most special musical ensembles in the world—notably because the group performs at such a high level but freely shares its talents with the community "for the love of music." I could think of no better way to celebrate that mission than by a collaboration with Koehler Books. Symphonicity is providing a state-of-the-art binaural recording of our *Messiah* Sing-Along performance to accompany the text of this book, *The Soul Feels Its Worth*.

The binaural recording technology will capture the musical magic as if the listener were physically present for the performance. Furthermore, by listening to our musical rendering while reading Hillery Schanck's devotional, the magic of Handel's *Messiah* can provide true meaning for the mind, heart, and soul.

We believe in the power of community, and we believe in the power of music. That's why Symphonicity exists. We love partnering with others to support their vision of community enhancement through the arts and letters. Together, our beliefs, our hard work, and our desire for sharing can improve the world and make a difference for future generations. For Symphonicity, this partnership of music and words is a perfect vehicle toward those goals. It is a high note in a song of community success. We believe it will ring true for many at home and around the world for years to come. We thank the Sandler Center Foundation Giving Circle for providing essential and generous support in bringing this recording to life. We especially thank Hillery Schanck and John Koehler for inviting us to be a part of this special experience.

And we thank you, too.

DANIEL W. BOOTHE
Music Director and Conductor
Symphonicity

INTRODUCTION

What Is Advent?

dvent is an ancient practice of using the season leading up to Christmas as a time of spiritual awakening. The Latin root of Advent means "coming" or "arrival" and refers to the coming of Christ. It's the traditional celebration of the First Coming of Jesus and the anxious awaiting and preparation of His second. The season is a time for remembering and rejoicing, watching and waiting, and reflecting upon the promises of God and anticipate the fulfillment of those promises with patience, prayer, and preparedness.

Practicing Advent helps us in several ways:

Advent helps us align our day calendars with the story of God. Many of us go on seasonal autopilot, spending more time thinking about the demands of the Christmas season than the glory of Christ. After Christmas, we can be left confused, wondering what happened and where the time went. An Advent experience helps us meaningfully connect the wonderful celebratory activities that fill our day with Jesus' gracious and radical intervention in the world.

Advent stirs our longings for the Second Coming of Christ. Even as we celebrate the incarnation of Jesus, Advent reminds us that though Christ's Kingdom is already present in the world (and in us!), it is also not yet fully realized. Thus, Advent stirs our hearts to pray for Christ's return, groan for the current brokenness of the world and in ourselves, and give ourselves more fully to participating in God's redemptive purposes in the world.

Advent gives us a strategic opportunity to share the hope of Christ's coming with our friends and family who are not connected to Jesus or the church. During the holidays, many people will consider coming to church and may be more open to talking about Jesus. We not only want to be available for these opportunities, but we also want to structure our lives to invite people into something more meaningful.

HANDEL'S *MESSIAH*

AS ADVENT?

Feeling the Story of God

*T*his devotional is based on the lyrics and music of Handel's *Messiah*. The lyrics of the production, otherwise known as the *libretto*, were all taken directly from Scripture and form an abridged, yet complete story of the Messiah, the Expected One of God. But incorporating the music can change the dynamic of our experience. Since music is felt, it allows us to more easily experience the emotion in the story of Jesus. Handel composed it to be just that way.

Unlike other devotional books, this one plays out like a story, but one in which *you* are participating. It begins with the ancient longing of Israel for its prophesied Messiah amidst a setting that was despairing and distressed. Then it transitions into first-century Palestine, where the "alleged" Messiah is born and lives. It carries on through Jesus' life, his execution, and his resurrection from the perspective of an onlooker seeking clarity and truth about His claims. It finishes with the growth of the early church, witnessing the final battle over death and the Day of Judgment, and finally, Jesus' glorification.

There will be days of celebration, and there will be days filled with sorrow and heaviness. Just like when you read a favorite story, a reader will suspend what is known about Christ and his ultimate deliverance so that the full purpose and understanding of the Messiah is felt. The point is to take you to these emotional places so that the full understanding and reception of the Messiah is felt. Suspend what you know for a moment and experience it in real time.

A deep spiritual encounter is in store as we praise God for his incarnation and cry expectantly with the church from all times, "Come quickly, Lord Jesus."

Handel's Messiah

HISTORY OF MESSIAH

eorge Frideric Handel composed *Messiah* in 1741. However, many people do not realize that it was a musical accompaniment to a libretto that had been assembled by Charles Jennens. A devout Christian, Jennens had previously written several librettos for Handel, but *Messiah* exclusively used Scripture references from the Bible.

We call it Handel's *Messiah*, but without the powerful arrangement of Jennens' texts, it could be argued that *Messiah* might not have been so lasting. A careful read of his libretto reveals the tremendous urgency Jennens had in the texts he chose for this oratorio. He meticulously assembled his biblical texts for *Messiah* to demonstrate that Jesus' life had been prophesied in the Old Testament. Jennens was clear in his objective: It was not just convention or tradition that made Christianity vital—Christianity was an eternal truth.

In July 1741, Jennens shared with Handel the libretto he had written so that Handel could complete the music for the oratorio. In a letter to his friend Edward Holdsworth, Jennens wrote: "*I hope [Handel] will lay out his whole Genius & Skill upon it, that the Composition may excel all his former Compositions, as the Subject excels every other Subject. The Subject is Messiah.*"

Handel began working on it on August 22 and completed the music for *Messiah* in just twenty-four days.

Each year at Christmastime, *Messiah* is performed in innumerable cities around the world and has become one of the best known and most popular choral works. It has been adapted over the years to accommodate large orchestral performances as well as large choirs. Handel wrote the original music for *Messiah* in a humbler mode than we hear today.

STRUCTURE OF MESSIAH

Messiah is made up of fifty-three *movements* divided into three parts and further subdivided into scenes.

- **Part I** begins with the prophecy of the Messiah and his virgin birth by several prophets, especially Isaiah.
- **Part II** covers the birth, life, death, resurrection, and ascension of the Messiah, as well as the later spreading of the Gospel.
- **Part III** concentrates on Paul's teaching of the resurrection of the dead and Christ's glorification in heaven.

As beautiful and uplifting as a grand performance of *Messiah* can be, this type of oratorio is meant to be a meditation, offering reflections on different aspects of the Messiah. This makes it ideal for a practice of Advent.

Why This Book Was Written

I grew up attending a very traditional Presbyterian church, but I did not become a believing Christian until my mid-twenties. When I did, I wanted to avoid the dry religious ceremony of my childhood. As I continued my spiritual journey, I gravitated toward nondenominational Christian churches that had shed the traditions of the denominations.

But later in life, I found myself craving some of the seasoned liturgy and practice that I remembered growing up.

Several years ago, I began researching the various ways that Advent had been practiced over the centuries. Among the traditional well-known Advent practices, I discovered others that I'd never heard of, among them using Handel's *Messiah* as an Advent tool. For several years, I experimented with using the *Messiah* as an Advent practice for myself leading up to Christmas. Music of all kinds has always deeply affected me.

I found it to be a quite wonderful, and sometimes emotional, way to prepare my heart for Christmas. I did not know whether this was an experience that others would enjoy, but I wanted so much for other people to experiment with it. I shared my original outline with others, but I found that many people simply needed a more extensive guide to get the benefit that I was getting.

So, here we are . . .

How to Use This Book

DAILY DEVOTIONAL

Use this guide as your daily devotional. It is set over twenty-five days, which is perfect for Christmas Advent. But it does not have to be limited to only that season of the year. Use it to draw closer to God and to reignite your relationship with Him.

PREPARE

The setup section is designed to give you some context about the Scriptures and prepare your heart to receive the words. It attempts to place you in the story.

TOPIC

Jennens arranged the libretto into scenes and topics. The topics are bolded.

READ, LISTEN, HEAR

My recommendation is to first read the passages. Absorb them as you normally would when you read Scripture. Then listen to the movements for each day while rereading the passages (libretto) in this guide.

The libretto for *Messiah* is all quoted from Scripture, both Old and New Testament, using the King James Version or the 1662 Book of Common Prayer. In some movements, multiple verses are blended. For instance, in some cases an Old Testament prophecy will be combined with the New Testament fulfillment of the prophecy. Sometimes the verses are abbreviated or connected to adjacent verses.

The Scripture in the movement is fully written out the way it is sung. In many cases, the verses are repeated and emphasized, allowing you to focus and meditate upon the words.

REFLECT AND FEEL

Pause and reflect on the feelings and the mood the music evokes. Using the list on the next page or in your own words, attempt to assign a specific emotion to the verses. Then contrast that emotion with your first reading. Consider how this emotion guides and changes your experience.

PRAYER

Use the prayer section as an opportunity to connect the Messiah Advent experience with your life. Continue to pray as the Holy Spirit guides you.

PALETTE OF EMOTIONS

The emotions below are set in a continuum from highest intensity to lowest.

Happy	Sad	Angry	Afraid	Ashamed
Elated	Depressed	Furious	Terrified	Sorrowful
Excited	Agonized	Enraged	Horrified	Remorseful
Overjoyed	Despondent	Outraged	Petrified	Defamed
Thrilled	Alone	Boiling	Scared	Worthless
Exuberant	Hurt	Irate	Fearful	Disgraced
Giddy	Dejected	Seething	Panicky	Dishonored
Ecstatic	Hopeless	Loathsome	Frantic	Mortified
Fired Up	Sorrowful	Betrayed	Shocked	Admonished
Passionate	Miserable	Upset	Desperate	Apologetic
Glorious	Heartbroken	Mad	Pleading	Unworthy
Harmonious	Upset	Defended	Frenetic	Sneaky
Confident	Somber	Frustrated	Threatened	Guilty
Cheerful	Lost	Incited	Apprehensive	Embarrassed
Gratified	Woeful	Agitated	Frightened	Secretive
Good	Distressed	Disgusted	Insecure	Bashful
Optimistic	Let down	Perturbed	Uneasy	Ridiculous
Encouraged	Melancholy	Annoyed	Intimidated	Regretful
Relieved	Gloomy	Uptight	Ominous	Uncomfortable
Satisfied	Unhappy	Resistant	Foreboding	Unsettled
Soothed	Moody	Irritated	Stressed out	Pitied

Happy	Sad	Angry	Afraid	Ashamed
Glowing	Blue	Touchy	Cautious	Silly
Glad	Disappointed		Nervous	
Sanguine	Dissatisfied		Worried	
Contented			Timid	
Pleasant			Unsure	
Tender			Anxious	
Pleased				
Mellow				
Nonchalant				

CHOOSING AND ACCESSING MUSIC

Literally hundreds of recordings of Handel's *Messiah* are available. Some choose to replicate Handel's simpler, humbler original version. Others are grander in style, with very large choirs and orchestras. There is no real perfect answer to choose and little to be risked in exploring and experimenting.

The real issue becomes access and simplicity. You will need to listen to different parts of the music on different days, and it may take a bit of organization in advance to keep it simple.

You could certainly listen to it on a CD player, but it will require you to physically be in the same location each time.

If you want to listen to it on your handheld device, it might present some minor obstacles. For instance, when playing *Messiah* on Spotify on my handheld device, it does not show the movement number and it abbreviates the name of the movement down to five characters. On iTunes, it shows the track number of the album, not the movement number, which is only useful for the first album. It also does not have room to show any letters from the name of the movement. This is what I see on Spotify and Apple iTunes for the identical performance:

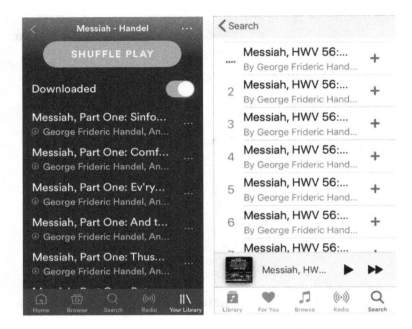

Scanning through fifty-three movements to find four letters of the name of a movement can be a difficult endeavor if you are not familiar with the names of the movements.

We offer you two simple options:

- Symphonicity has graciously created a binaural recording of their live performance of the *Messiah* symphony, which you can access online.
- Or if you would prefer to use Spotify, playlists have been created for each day to simplify the issue above.

Both options can be found here:

http://themessiahadvent.com/access-the-music/

As a feature of convenience, a QR code is embedded into each day's devotion, which allows you to quickly navigate to the music for each day by using the camera on your smartphone or a QR reader.

Lectio Divina

*Y*ou can also use this guide as a *Lectio Divina*. Lectio Divina is an ancient practice that promotes an immediate union with God by slowly meditating on Scripture and inviting the Holy Spirit to talk to you about what is necessary for you to learn, know, or do from the Scripture. More than simply *studying* Scripture, Lectio Divina is a relational interaction with His Word with your body, mind, heart, and your spirit. Here is an example of how to practice Lectio Divina.

PREPARATION

In the guide, turn to the specific day of Advent upon which you will be meditating. Prepare your audio device by finding the corresponding movement(s) from Handel's *Messiah* that you will be listening to that day.

FIRST READING/LISTENING

Quiet yourself and **pray** that the Holy Spirit will guard your heart and guide your meditation.

Listen to the movements and read the passages.

Silently reflect on these passages before God for one minute, simply acquainting yourself with them and the meaning of the words. At this point, make no judgments or conclusions; just let the passages be the single focus of your quieted mind.

SECOND READING

Pray that God will bring a single word or phrase to your conscious mind.

Without the music, **read** the passage slowly, out loud. Listen for whatever God uses to capture your attention in the passage or in your inner experience.

Silently reflect on this word or phrase before God for one minute. Consider the various meanings and its context.

THIRD READING

Pray first that God will guide you in understanding how this word or passage connects with your life.

Read the passage slowly, out loud.

Silently reflect on this word or phrase before God for three to five minutes. Listen to how the passage seems to touch your life experience.

FOURTH READING

Pray first that God will reveal to you why He used this word or phrase for this moment.

Read the passage slowly, out loud.

Silently reflect on this word or phrase before God for three to five minutes. Consider the following questions: What do you feel the passage might be inviting you to do? What is God inviting you to be? How is God inviting you to change?

CONCLUDE

Spend some time in **prayer** over what you received from God's Word, and **give thanks** for His gift to you.

THE MEDITATIONS

"... the Subject excels every other Subject.
The Subject is Messiah."

—Charles Jennens

(in his letter to Handel about producing *Messiah*)

DAY 1

The Hopes and Fear of All the Years

Then you shall call, and the Lord will answer;
You will cry, and he will say, 'Here I am.'

Isaiah 58:9

• DAY 1 MUSIC •
https://themessiahadvent.com/day-1/

PREPARE

"Isaiah's prophecy of salvation"

Throughout their history, the people of Israel suffered greatly, both for their own sin and because of their oppression by others. Their land was frequently overrun by foreign powers who knew the strategic significance of Palestine, which connected Africa, Europe, and Asia. They suffered under slavery in Egypt and endured the troubles of exile. In short, they were a people in desperate need of consolation and comfort.

The Israelites clung tightly to the promises that the Messiah would one day level life's inequities and establish righteousness throughout His earthly kingdom. They wondered when the Son of David would arrive to guard them and provide for the forgiveness of their sin. He could not arrive soon enough.

We can relate to their desire for consolation. Even as we celebrate the incarnation of the Messiah, we are quickly reminded that though His Kingdom is already present in the world, it is also not yet fully realized. And for us, consolation is also contingent upon His return.

READ, LISTEN, HEAR

No 1   **Symphony**

No 2   **Recitative (Tenor)**

"Comfort ye, comfort ye My people,
Saith your God.
Speak ye comfortably to Jerusalem,
and cry unto her, that her warfare is accomplished,
That her iniquity is pardoned,
The voice of him that crieth
in the wilderness;
'Prepare ye the way of the Lord;
Make straight in the desert
a highway for our God.'"

Isaiah 40:1-3

No 3   **Aria (Tenor)**

"Every valley shall be exalted,
And every mountain and hill made low:
the crooked straight,
And the rough places plain."

Isaiah 40:4

No 4   **Chorus**

"And the glory of the Lord shall be revealed,
and all flesh shall see it together:
For the mouth of the Lord hath spoken it."

Isaiah 40:5

REFLECT AND FEEL

What emotions flowed out of today's devotional?

How did these emotions guide your experience of the Scripture?

PRAYER

Father,

I need you. As I settle into the beginning of this Advent experience, it reminds me that I am also waiting . . . waiting for your return. How much longer, Lord? How much longer will you allow this world to pursue the path that it chooses? I wonder about this.

Comfort me, Lord. Tell me again of Your promises when I worry. And I worry about . . .

DAY 2

The Frightening Prerequisite to Righteousness

Alas, you who are longing for the day of the Lord,
for what purpose will the day of the Lord be to you?
It will be darkness and not light.

Amos 5:18

• DAY 2 MUSIC •

https://themessiahadvent.com/day-2/

PREPARE

"The prophecy of the coming of Messiah and the question of what this may portend for the World"

The words of the prophet Zephaniah should cause us to pause . . .

> On the day of the Lord's wrath;
> And all the earth will be devoured
> In the fire of His jealousy,
> For He will make a complete end,
> Indeed a terrifying one,
> Of all the inhabitants of the earth.

Zephaniah 1:18

Zephaniah refers to the day of the Lord's wrath—Yahweh's judgment of mankind. For us, His words are frightening and yet unavoidable. How do we view this day of the Lord? What does it actually mean for the world? For me?

God will purify His people and return us to righteousness. The result is glorious, but the process of purification is painful.

We know in our spirit that there is impurity within ourselves that must be dealt with. What will purification look and feel like?

LISTEN, HEAR, FEEL

No 5   **Recitative (Bass)**

Thus saith the Lord of Hosts;
Yet once, a little while
and I will shake the heavens, and the earth,
and the sea, and the dry land;
And I will shake all nations,
and the desire of all nations shall come.

Haggai 2:6-7

The Lord, whom ye seek,
shall suddenly come to His temple,
even the messenger of the Covenant,
whom ye delight in;
behold, He shall come, saith the Lord of hosts.

Malachi 3:1

No 6   **Aria (Bass)**

But who may abide the Day of His Coming?
and who shall stand when He appeareth?
For He is like a refiner's fire.

Malachi 3:2

No 7   **Chorus**

And He shall purify the sons of Levi . . .
that they may offer unto the Lord
an offering in righteousness.

Malachi 3:3

REFLECT AND FEEL

What emotions flowed out of today's devotional?

How did these emotions guide your experience of the Scripture?

PRAYER

Father,

I realize that purification is necessary for me. I confess that by my own daily thoughts and actions, I have fallen way short of Your expectations and hopes. But if I am honest, this makes me worry because of the manner in which your prophets describe this process. How will I possibly survive purification? What will become of me?

Something else perplexes me. How is it that you can call me holy and righteous in Scripture when I have not yet undergone purification? How can I be holy and also do the things I do? . . .

DAY 3

A Mysterious Hope

"Behold, days are coming," declares the Lord,
"when I will make a new covenant with the house of
Israel and with the house of Judah."

Jeremiah 31:31

• DAY 3 MUSIC •

https://themessiahadvent.com/day-3/

PREPARE

"The prophecy of the virgin birth" (Part 1)

As we wait, a vestige of hope appears on the horizon. A prophet of God tells us that a virgin will bear a son. This mysterious miracle is to be a sign that this baby will be "God with us."

God with us.

God is sending his Son to come and rescue us from our troubles. That future promise is such good news that we are told to go and proclaim it . . . today.

It is both encouraging and mysterious. How can we be sure that it will happen as promised? Is it enough to know what God says about this promise to trust that it will be as He says? How do we know *when* we will be rescued?

LISTEN, HEAR, FEEL

No 8   **Recitative (Alto)**

Behold, a virgin shall conceive, and bear a Son,
and shall call his name EMMANUEL,
God with us.

Isaiah 7:14 (Matthew 1:23)

No 9   **Aria (Alto)**

O thou that tellest good tidings to Zion,
get thee up into the high mountain;
O thou that tellest good tidings to Jerusalem,
lift up thy voice with strength;
lift it up, be not afraid;
say unto the cities of Judah,
"Behold your God!"

Isaiah 40:9

Chorus

Arise, shine; for thy light is come,
and the glory of the Lord is risen upon thee

Isaiah 60:1

REFLECT AND FEEL

What emotions flowed out of today's devotional?

How did these emotions guide your experience of the Scripture?

PRAYER

Father,

I do believe your Word is truth . . . and I want to depend on you completely. But it is hard for me to always trust that you are in control when I witness some of the things that happen in the world and in my life. I confess that I sometimes question whether you truly love me or whether you have my best interests in mind when circumstances don't go my way.

I don't like admitting this, but it's hard for me to believe all your promises. I want to, but I just don't. Please give me the faith to overcome my doubts. Please allow me to walk through life with confidence, especially in these areas that I struggle with trusting you in the most . . .

DAY 4

Light Has Driven out the Darkness

"This is the judgment,
that the Light has come into the world,
and men loved the darkness rather than the Light,
for their deeds were evil.
For everyone who does evil hates the Light,
and does not come to the Light
for fear that his deeds will be exposed.
But he who practices the truth comes to the Light,
so that his deeds may be manifested
as having been wrought in God."

John 3:19-21

• DAY 4 MUSIC •

https://themessiahadvent.com/day-4/

PREPARE

"The prophecy of the virgin birth" (Part 2)

In our present state, it is dark around us and it is hard to see clearly. After groping around for a long time, we realize that we have been walking around aimlessly in a barren desert. The problem: We have become used to this environment and in some ways, we have simply adapted to this as our norm.

We strive to do good because we want to please God. But over time we have become very aware that even our sincerest effort is just not enough. We try and we try, but all the while we watch as we dump new wheelbarrows full of sin each day that thwart any chance of keeping us in good standing before God.

But today, amid this ominous darkness, we feel a hint of something different, something new. God is up to something . . . something very good. It begins with this baby but somehow seems to involve me.

LISTEN, HEAR, FEEL

No 10   Recitative (Bass)

> For, behold, darkness shall cover the earth,
>   and gross darkness the people;
> but the Lord shall arise upon thee
>   and His glory shall be seen upon thee.
> And the Gentiles shall come to thy light,
>   and kings to the brightness of thy rising.

Isaiah 60:2-3

No 11   Aria (Bass)

> The people that walked in darkness
>   have seen a great light:
> and they that dwell in the land of the
>   shadow of death,
>   upon them hath the light shined.

Isaiah 9:2 (Matthew 3:16)

No. 12   Chorus

> For unto us a Child is born,
>   unto us a Son is given:
>   and the government shall be upon His
>   shoulder:
> and His name shall be called
>   Wonderful, Counsellor,
>   the mighty God,
>   the everlasting Father,
>   the Prince of Peace.

Isaiah 9:6

REFLECT AND FEEL

What emotions flowed out of today's devotional?

How did these emotions guide your experience of the Scripture?

PRAYER

Father,

I understand about darkness. I see it, sense it, and feel it all around me. It frightens me. But even more frightening is the darkness I witness inside of me. I hate it because it is so familiar. I hate it because it leads me away from you. As hard as I have tried, I know that I cannot atone for these sins on my own. Striving to "do good" just leads me back to the mouth of the river where these dark secrets began. In this moment, I confess these shadowy sins that cause me to turn away from you . . .

DAY 5

Peace Breaks Through

"This will be a sign for you:
you will find a baby wrapped in cloths
and lying in a manger."

Luke 2:12

• DAY 5 MUSIC •

https://themessiahadvent.com/day-5/

PREPARE

"The appearance of the Angels to the Shepherds"

On a quiet night in Bethlehem, in an ordinary field, the Eternal punctures time and space and reality is invaded. In that moment, thousand-year-old prophecies cease being mythical divinations and become precursors of an actual historical event.

This herald of heaven could have appeared in many places:

> To the kings in their palaces . . .
> To the religious leaders in the temple court . . .
> To the scholars in the forum . . .
> To the business leaders in the marketplace . . .

But this angelic flash mob was summoned to a small outpost of lowly shepherds in the middle of the night. The shepherds' reactions may not have been ideal, but they were authentic. The supernatural has always been one of our greatest mysteries and our greatest fears.

This mystical interruption did not come to scare but instead to deliver good news of the greatest joy.

LISTEN, HEAR, FEEL

No 13   Pifa—Shepherding Symphony

No 14   Recitative (Soprano)

There were shepherds abiding in the field,
keeping watch over their flocks by night.

Luke 2:8

No 15   Recitative (Soprano)

And lo! the angel of the Lord came upon them,
and the glory of the Lord shone round about them:
 and they were sore afraid.

Luke 2:9

And the angel said unto them, "Fear not; for
behold, I bring you good tidings of great joy,
which shall be to all people. For unto you is born
this day in the city of David a Saviour, which is
Christ the Lord."

Luke 2:10-11

No 16   Recitative (Soprano)

And suddenly there was with the angel a
multitude of the heavenly host praising God,
and saying:

Luke 2:13

No 17   Chorus
"Glory to God in the highest, and peace
on earth, good will towards men."

Luke 2:14

REFLECT AND FEEL

What emotions flowed out of today's devotional?

How did these emotions guide your experience of the Scripture?

PRAYER

Father,

Today I am reminded of your very real presence with me right now. You have certainly entered my world. I confess that I often fail to remember the miraculous ways you have made yourself known to me. Even in my darkness, you are here. Remind me, again, of the instances that I have forgotten. I thank you as I recall these bright realities that are, even now, shining on and in me . . .

DAY 6

The Testimony of Miracles

The news about Him spread throughout all Syria,
and they brought to him all who were ill,
those suffering with various diseases and pains,
demoniacs, epileptics, paralytics; and He healed them.

Matthew 4:24-25

Then it happened that as Jesus was reclining at the table
in the house, behold, many tax collectors and sinners
came and were dining with Jesus and His disciples.

Matthew 9:10

He said to the paralytic—"I say to you, get up,
and pick up your stretcher and go home."
Immediately he got up before them,
and picked up what he had been lying on,
and went home glorifying God.
They were all struck with astonishment
and began glorifying God;
and they were filled with fear, saying,
"We have seen remarkable things today."

Luke 5:24-26

• DAY 6 MUSIC •
https://themessiahadvent.com/day-6/

PREPARE

"Christ's redemptive miracles on earth" (Part 1)

Jesus' active ministry of teaching emphasized that the kingdom of God was at hand and that He was truly the Messiah promised by the prophets. His many miracles served as signs—signs to allow the nation of Israel to come to a correct decision regarding his Messianic claim, then repent, and believe. When witnessing His miracles, many were astonished and glorified God. However, others were fearful and some were mad. The implications of His power and authority disrupted the lives they had built for themselves.

LISTEN, HEAR, FEEL

No 18   **Aria (Soprano)**

Rejoice greatly, O daughter of Zion;
Shout, O daughter of Jerusalem:
behold, thy King cometh unto thee.
He is the righteous Saviour.
And he shall speak peace unto the heathen.

Zechariah 9:9-10 (Matthew 21:5)

No 19   **Recitative (Alto)**

Then the eyes of the blind shall be opened, and the ears of
the deaf shall be unstopped. Then shall the lame man leap as
an hart, and the tongue of the dumb shall sing.

Isaiah 35:5-6

REFLECT AND FEEL

What emotions flowed out of today's devotional?

How did these emotions guide your experience of the Scripture?

PRAYER

Father,

I have the benefit of all the Scriptures as well as access to an endless supply of books written about Your Word. Unfortunately, this is a double-edged sword for me. Because I have read about Your miracles over and over, I must admit that my sense of wonder and astonishment about You has waned.

You healed a man. You cured a woman. A man now sees. A man now walks. Yet, if I myself had witnessed any of these, it would have been life-changing for me.

Lord, I don't need more knowledge about You. What I need is to regain my sense of fear and amazement.

When I meditate on the miracles that I have witnessed or read about, where does it lead me? Am I distracted by my own plans and pursuits, or do I fall at Your feet and worship You? Do your miracles convince me of Your Messiahship? As a result, do I allow You to truly be my King, or do I prefer to sit on the throne myself?

DAY 7

Try Harder or Trust?

Therefore they said to Him,
"What shall we do,
so that we may work the works of God?"
Jesus answered and said to them,
"This is the work of God,
that you believe in Him whom He has sent."

John 6:28-29

• DAY 7 MUSIC •

https://themessiahadvent.com/day-7/

PREPARE

"Christ's redemptive miracles on earth" (Part 2)

Somehow, somewhere along the way, we fixated on the idea that to be right with God, it was incumbent upon us to get our acts together. We have tried everything. We have tried connecting to Him better through daily devotionals and through Bible reading plans. We have given more money and volunteered. We have tried our best to be "good Christians." We have committed our lives to Him . . . then recommitted . . . then recommitted. Yet, we seem to get nowhere and we are totally exhausted.

But this alleged Messiah suggests something different. Instead of asking us to commit, He invites us to submit; to be able to come under Him for the purpose of protection. He wants this for us because He loves us. Whereas commitment is an act of will and effort, submitting is an act of faith. The problem is that to us, submit seems to imply an opponent, a fight, and ultimately a defeat, which is just not the case.

But God offers a totally different proposal. His reassuring words call us to simply draw near. He simply wants us to trust Him. He even tells us there is no such thing as a "good Christian."

READ, LISTEN, HEAR

No 20   Aria (Alto)

He shall feed his flock like a shepherd;
and he shall gather the lambs with His arm,
and carry them in His bosom,
and shall gently lead those that are with young.

Isaiah 40:11

Come unto [Him],
all ye that labour and are heavy laden,
and [He shall] give you rest.
Take [His] yoke upon you,
and learn of [Him];
for [He is] meek and lowly of heart:
and ye shall find rest unto your souls.

Matthew 11:28-29

No 21   Chorus

[His] yoke is easy,
and [His] burden is light.

Matthew 11:30

REFLECT AND FEEL

What emotions flowed out of today's devotional?

How did these emotions guide your experience of the Scripture?

PRAYER

Father,

Trusting is not easy for me. Yielding is even harder. Every aspect of life seems to require effort, endurance, and ability. Even freedom is fought for and earned.

Yet, you tell me something completely different. You call me to your arms and promise me freedom by yielding to You. You promise peace and life when I give up trying to gain these very things by my own effort. Can that really be true?

Maybe that is why the yoke that I have upon me is neither easy nor light. Where did I get this yoke, if it is not Yours? For You to be my one, true King, there are some other kings I worship that I need your help to release. And they are . . .

DAY 8

Lambs, Blood, and Deliverance

The [lamb's] blood shall be a sign for you
on the houses where you live;
and when I see the blood I will pass over you.

Exodus 12:13

• DAY 8 MUSIC •

https://themessiahadvent.com/day-8/

PREPARE

"The redemptive sacrifice" (Part 1)

Before the Israelites' notorious escape from Egypt, the Lord instructed them to spread the blood of a sacrificed lamb over their doorposts so that the angel of death would "pass over" their home and save them. For centuries since then, the blood of hundreds of thousands of lambs was spilled in the temple each year to pay the price for the sins of the people. The people of Israel well understood the method by which God accounted for their sin.

We need to understand this as well. For our sins to be covered, a price must be paid . . . with a sacrifice of blood. You get to choose: *your life* or *the lamb's*. It is messy; it is violent; and it is brutal.

And then, in the Judean wilderness, a voice . . .

John the Baptist appears on the scene after spending most of his life in the wilderness, far away from the religion of his day. Appointed by God, he is the herald to the King, ensuring that when the Messiah comes, we are prepared and we believe. God tells John, "When one comes to you, and you see the Holy Spirit descending and remaining on Him like a dove, this is the One for whom you are waiting." The next day, Jesus came to him and John proclaimed something both shocking and incredible to us.

READ, LISTEN, HEAR

No 22   **Chorus**

Behold the Lamb of God,
that taketh away the sins of the world.

John 1:29

REFLECT AND FEEL

What emotions flowed out of today's devotional?

How did these emotions guide your experience of the Scripture?

PRAYER

Father,

Today, I am struck by a great paradox: Your yoke is light for me, yet my burden on You is quite heavy.

You have taken the weight of all my sin and exchanged it for the freedom and delight of walking with You. But not just for me . . . for the whole world! What can I say? Why, Lord? What is it about me that makes this worth it for You?

My heart leaps at this good news, and yet I simultaneously grieve, contemplating the gravity of what is truly at stake . . .

DAY 9

Misunderstood and Rejected

"O Jerusalem, Jerusalem, the city that kills the prophets
and stones those sent to her!
How often I wanted to gather your children together,
just as a hen gathers her brood under her wings,
and you would not have it!"

Luke 13:34

• DAY 9 MUSIC •

https://themessiahadvent.com/day-9/

PREPARE

"The redemptive sacrifice" (Part 2)

Over thousands of years, the people of God manipulated what God intended for them into a fully operational, and dysfunctional, religious system. Spirituality became a ladder of righteousness, with the expectation that participants would climb their way to God.

However, there was one problem. Achieving righteousness was never even possible for us. To make matters worse, righteousness is particularly hard work. Nevertheless, in an attempt to prevail against this endless loop, rules were strengthened. Stricter laws were established, with innumerable boundaries around them to prevent even accidental violations. The bar was set high. Bootstraps were pulled tight. However, this just made spiritual living more burdensome, more tiring, and more guilt inducing.

Because human beings are resourceful though, we identified a glitch in the system and immediately capitalized on it. We found that by simply appearing righteous to others, we could feel safe.

Then, out of nowhere, this man comes along and starts calling out my hypocrisy. Jesus used these words about me: "You are like a whitewashed tomb which on the outside appears beautiful, but inside you are full of dead men's bones." Suddenly, in this light, I don't look so good. Jesus exposes my duplicity for all to see, which is embarrassing and humiliating. I look over my shoulder and notice others whispering to one other. What if they find out?! *It does not take a genius to figure out that something must be done about this Jesus fellow*, we think. *This just won't do.*

READ, LISTEN, HEAR

No 23   **Aria (Alto)**

He was despised and rejected of men:
a man of sorrows, and acquainted with grief.

Isaiah 53:3

[He] gave [His] back to the smiters,
and [His] cheeks to them that plucked off the hair:
[He] hid not [His] face from shame and spitting.

Isaiah 50:6

REFLECT AND FEEL

What emotions flowed out of today's devotional?

How did these emotions guide your experience of the Scripture?

PRAYER

Father,

Why does your plan involve you stripping me of the reputation that I have carefully built? Privately, I enjoy being with you, but when you expose me to others . . . well, that just makes me want to go away.

Deep down, I am suspicious of others. I know they have their problems, depravities, and weaknesses, but mine feel worse and certainly more shameful. I am afraid that if everyone knew the real me, I would be rejected. So instead I turn away from you and return to this religious system that at least I understand and know how to manipulate for my safety.

It is ironic that the thing I fear the most is being despised and rejected. Yet, that is exactly what happens to You when I avoid You.

So for a fleeting moment, I can relate to the scorn you endured and how that must have felt. Help me understand that better . . .

DAY 10

Sheep

In those days there was no king in Israel;
every man did what was right in his own eyes.

Judges 17:6

"Father, forgive them;
for they do not know what they are doing."

Luke 23:34

• DAY 10 MUSIC •

https://themessiahadvent.com/day-10/

PREPARE

"The scourging"

"I have my truth and you have your truth."
"A person can do whatever she wants as long as it doesn't hurt anyone else."
"I am the master of my fate. I am the captain of my soul."
"It's my world, and you're just living in it."
"I did it my way."

These are slogans of today's culture. We say them; we believe them; we live them. We strive for freedom, power, and wealth, and we admire the self-made. We impulsively chase what we desire with single-minded determination. And we bristle at any authority, rules, or wisdom that oppose our wishes. Not surprisingly, our stubborn independence and resolve breed a sense of heroicism in us. And in the age of social media, we feel justified by finger touch "likes" and mutually take comfort in the pursuit of whatever brings us pleasure.

God has a word for people like us:

Sheep.

READ, LISTEN, HEAR

No 24   Chorus

Surely he hath borne our griefs,
and carried our sorrows.
He was wounded for our transgressions,
he was bruised for our iniquities:
the chastisement of our peace was upon him

Isaiah 53:4-5

No 25   Chorus

and with His stripes we are healed

Isaiah 53:5b

No 26   Chorus

All we like sheep have gone astray;
we have turned every one to his own way;
and the Lord hath laid on him
the iniquity of us all.

Isaiah 53:6

REFLECT AND FEEL

What emotions flowed out of today's devotional?

How did these emotions guide your experience of the Scripture?

PRAYER

Father,

I confess that I want to be my own king. I try to control my world around me, but I am not the master of destiny that I imagine. I even pick and choose the things about You that I will follow or cast aside. I wander all over the place, far away from the guidance and wisdom that You readily make available to me, and I feel safe because I see others wandering with me. What makes this worse is that I am simply unaware of the danger most of the time. I admit now that I am weak and defenseless against all types of predators.

I am a sheep.

But, I am reminded that You are a Shepherd . . . a Good Shepherd. And I am beginning to see that the consequence of my life ultimately falls on You, the very One who saves me. Each lash You receive can be traced back to my life, and yet it is those very same lashes that heal me.

Father, have mercy on me. Help me listen for your voice. Help me follow your calls and not wander. Lead me. Restore me. Guide me. Comfort me. Anoint me. I want to dwell in your house . . . forever.

DAY 11

The Root of Bitterness

Now there was also an inscription above Him,
"THIS IS THE KING OF THE JEWS."

Luke 23:38

Then they spat in His face
and beat Him with their fists;
and others slapped Him.

Matthew 26:67

So then, you will know them by their fruits.

Matthew 7:20

• DAY 11 MUSIC •

https://themessiahadvent.com/day-11/

PREPARE

"The agony on the cross" (Part 1)

When Jesus hung on the cross, everyone mocked and rejected him—the religious leaders as well as the civic leaders; the guards; the criminals hanging next to Jesus; people just passing by. They were all hoping for something from Him. Seeing Him dying on the cross was the proof they needed to confirm that He was not able to deliver for them.

When Jesus failed to provide what they wanted and the way in which they wanted it, it caused a root of bitterness to take hold in their hearts. They had a wrong understanding of Jesus and a wrong view of eternal security. They wanted to continue to walk in life according to their own perspective and rules.

READ, LISTEN, HEAR

No 27   Recitative (Tenor)

All they that see [Him] laugh [Him] to scorn:
they shoot out their lips,
they shake their heads,
saying:

Psalm 22:7

No 28   Chorus

He trusted [in God]
that He would deliver Him:
let Him deliver Him,
if He delight in Him.

Psalm 22:8 (Matthew 27:43)

REFLECT AND FEEL

What emotions flowed out of today's devotional?

How did these emotions guide your experience of the Scripture?

PRAYER

Father,

I confess that I also have expectations for You. Sometimes when I have been most desperate, I have prayed to You and You did not answer. Other times, You did not answer my prayers the way I wanted. I confess that I can begin to wonder, *What kind of God are You? Don't You care about me?*

Roots of bitterness have sprung in me also. And the fruit of that in my life is not pretty. In fact, it is downright poisonous. My sinful responses to things that have happened to me are buried deeply within me. Can we talk about them? . . .

DAY 12

Despair

Then He said to them,
"My soul is deeply grieved, to the point of death;
remain here and keep watch with Me."

Matthew 26:38

"Simon, are you asleep?
Could you not keep watch for one hour?"

Mark 14:37

And they all left Him and fled.

Mark 14:50

Jesus cried out with a loud voice, saying,
"Eli, Eli, lama sabachthani?" that is,
"My God, My God, why have You forsaken Me?"

Matthew 27:46

• **DAY 12 MUSIC** •

https://themessiahadvent.com/day-12/

PREPARE

"The agony on the cross" (Part 2)

Contrary to what people might believe, the extreme grief that Jesus experiences is not focused upon himself. When Jesus was approaching Jerusalem, he began weeping over it, saying, "If you had known in this day, even you, the things which make for peace! But now they have been hidden from your eyes."

He longs for *our* rescue and redemption.

Jesus knows that Israel's rejection of his Messianic claims and its failure to respond to his invitation are about to be permanently sealed. His death will bring forth God's judgment and the destruction of Jerusalem and the temple, just as he had warned and lamented.

Our failure, like the three disciples whom he asked to watch and pray, demonstrates that not even his most intimate associates have the spiritual discernment to understand what is happening. And, for that, He despairs.

READ, LISTEN, HEAR

No 29   **Recitative (Tenor)**

[Thy] rebuke hath broken [His] heart;
[He is] full of heaviness.
[He] looked for some to have pity [on Him],
but there was no man;
neither found [He] any to comfort [Him].

Psalm 69:20

No 30   **Arioso (Soprano)**

Behold, and see if there be any sorrow
like unto [His] sorrow.

Lamentations 1:12

REFLECT AND FEEL

What emotions flowed out of today's devotional?

How did these emotions guide your experience of the Scripture?

PRAYER

Father,

I admit that I can't begin to understand Your purposes. Even when I believe that I know what You are doing, I find that I simply do not. I just don't think the way You do.

Your grief over the path we have chosen demonstrates how much You love people.

What I am beginning to realize is that Your heart is broken because "my ways" prevent me from experiencing all You have for me. "My ways" prevent me from loving You and loving others the way You designed me to do so. "My ways" prevent me from living "life to the full."

Ironically, I tend to blame my outcomes on You and Your goodness rather than on me and my actions. Allow Your grief to guide me to see "my ways" more clearly and how far they are from Your ways . . .

DAY 13

Death: The End of Suffering

He said, "It is finished!"
And He bowed His head and gave up His spirit.

John 19:30

• DAY 13 MUSIC •

https://themessiahadvent.com/day-13/

PREPARE

"His sacrificial death, His passage through Hell and Resurrection"

After the long drawn-out description and detail of Jesus' torture and suffering, we enter the quiet calm of His death.

The night is over.

Similar to the demons that Jesus silenced, Jesus does not allow death much of a voice. That is because death was no master over Him. Death was simply His last enemy, and He abolished it. In some ways, He appears to mock his adversary: "Death, where is your victory? Where is your sting?"

The perishable has just put on the imperishable.

Morning has begun.

READ, LISTEN, HEAR

No 31   Recitative (Tenor)

> He was cut off out of the land of the living:
> for the transgression of [Thy] people
> *was He stricken.*

Isaiah 53:8

No 32   Aria (Tenor)

> [But] thou [didst] not leave [His] soul in hell;
> nor [didst] thou suffer Thy Holy One
> to see corruption.

Psalm 16:10 (Acts 2:27)

REFLECT AND FEEL

What emotions flowed out of today's devotional?

How did these emotions guide your experience of the Scripture?

PRAYER

Father,

It is hard for me not to obsess about death from my perspective. I scan the horizon as far as I can see. It has an unavoidable steep cliff at its end. This is the world I know, the life I know. What am I to think?

Because of my inability to see beyond death as I know it, I live with a scarcity mentality. I frenetically run after everything in life that I want because I am afraid that it will run out. I am desperate to accomplish all that I desire, because each time I look up to the horizon, I notice that I am markedly closer to the cliff. This distracts me from You and Your purposes.

But to whom else shall I go? You have the words of eternal life. Your words give me pictures of what lies beyond the horizon. You talk about life with fullness and purpose and abundance. You tell a story much greater than I can conceive.

Jesus, Your few words about death put life in perspective for me. They remind me that death was not the end for You, nor is it the end for me. It is simply a doorway. Help me trust what You say about the doorway and beyond, and release my hands upon the things I grip so tightly . . .

DAY 14

Glory Has a King

And His voice was like the sound of many waters;
and the earth shone with His glory.

Ezekiel 43:2

• DAY 14 MUSIC •

https://themessiahadvent.com/day-14/

PREPARE

"His ascension"

David, after being anointed king over all of Israel, fought a battle against the Philistines protecting the newly acquired Jerusalem, which was renamed the City of David.

David built God's city there on Mount Zion and prepared a great reception for the Ark of the Covenant, the very presence of God, bringing it to its final resting place.

Now, a thousand years later, after Jesus' defeat over death, this King of ours ascends to His rightful place and there is also a great procession. The royal entrance has begun.

READ, LISTEN, HEAR

No 33   **Chorus**

Lift up your heads, O ye gates;
and be ye lift up, ye everlasting doors;
and the King of Glory shall come in.
Who is this King of Glory?
The Lord strong and mighty,
the Lord mighty in battle.
Lift up your heads, O ye gates;
and be ye lift up, ye everlasting doors;
and the King of Glory shall come in.
Who is this King of Glory?
The Lord of Hosts,
He is the King of Glory.

Psalm 24:7-10

REFLECT AND FEEL

What emotions flowed out of today's devotional?

How did these emotions guide your experience of the Scripture?

PRAYER

Father,

You are the King of Glory.

All I can do today is bow before you and behold Your beauty. What was impossible for us to do on our own, You have accomplished with Your power and might. You have defeated death for mankind.

Jesus, I see what you have done and I receive the gift of Your Kingship over me. Today, You receive my heart as well as my will. I will choose to trust You with all aspects of my life.

Lord, I pray that Your glory will be demonstrated in my life:

  to my family, including . . .
  to my friends, including . . .
  and to the world around me.

DAY 15

A Rightful Reception

So that at the name of Jesus EVERY KNEE WILL BOW,
of those who are in heaven and on earth
and under the earth.

Philippians 2:10

• DAY 15 MUSIC •

https://themessiahadvent.com/day-15/

PREPARE

God discloses his identity in heaven

As Jesus ascends back to heaven, the reception begins. First, the angels of God greet Him. Angels are creations of God. They are spiritual beings who act as God's agents and messengers to accomplish His purposes. They understand their relationship to Him. They do not think of themselves more highly than they ought.

We are creations of God too. We, however, struggle with our relationship.

Jesus, though, is altogether distinct. He is begotten, which means He is not created by God, but instead, He is of God . . . He is God. And Jesus has a relationship also. He humbled himself to take on the physical nature of a human so that He could be a substitute for the due price of our waywardness.

Once we understand who Jesus is, we begin to understand our relationship to God. When we understand our relationship, we will naturally bow.

Some of us will simply recognize Him for who He is. Others will need to be convinced. Either way, at some point, we will all bow because He will not go unrecognized.

The angels bowed because they knew the name of the Begotten One.

READ, LISTEN, HEAR

No 34   **Recitative (Tenor)**

For unto which of the angels said He at any time,
Thou art my Son, this day have I begotten thee?

Hebrews 1:5 (Psalm 2:7)

No 35   **Chorus**

Let all the angels of God worship Him.

Hebrews 1:6

REFLECT AND FEEL

What emotions flowed out of today's devotional?

How did these emotions guide your experience of the Scripture?

PRAYER

Father,

I was designed to worship. My desire is, like the angels, to worship You.

I realize, however, that I worship other things as well . . . things not worthy of my worship. What is it about these things that draw my adoration and devotion? What is it inside me that causes me to bow down before them instead of You?

They enslave me. You free me.

Reveal in me everything that distracts from the reality that You, Jesus, are the Begotten One and the only one worthy of all glory.
Help me name the charlatan kings to which I so often give my allegiance . . .

DAY 16

Gifts for the Temple

"But this is the covenant which I will make
with the house of Israel after those days,"
declares the Lord,
"I will put My law within them
and on their heart I will write it;
and I will be their God, and they shall be My people."

Jeremiah 31:33

And suddenly there came from heaven
a noise like a violent rushing wind,
and it filled the whole house where they were sitting.
And there appeared to them tongues as of fire distribut-
ing themselves, and the rested on each one of them.
And they were all filled with the Holy Spirit
and began to speak with other tongues,
as the Spirit was giving them utterance.

Acts 2:2-4

• DAY 16 MUSIC •
https://themessiahadvent.com/day-16/

PREPARE

"Whitsun" [Pentecost]

When the ark was carried up Mount Zion and set in its permanent place among God's people, the singers would likely have celebrated with this psalm of David.

God had triumphed over His enemies and had accumulated the rewards of the conquered to be used for the building of the temple in Jerusalem. Yet, this event, like many others, was figurative and pointed to a future reality for God's people.

God had spoken to His people through the prophets many times, reminding them, *"I will be their God, and they shall be My people."*

After binding the strong one and redeeming human nature from the grave, Jesus carries it all to the throne of God. The gifts Jesus then received from His Heavenly Father, gifts of the spirit, He now passes on to us to build up the new temple of the living God . . . you and me . . . the permanent place.

"I will be [your] God, and [you] shall be My people."

READ, LISTEN, HEAR

No 36   **Aria (Bass)**

Thou art gone up on high,
Thou hast led captivity captive,
and received gifts for men;
yea, even for Thine enemies,
that the Lord God might dwell among them.

Psalm 68:18 (Ephesians 4:8)

REFLECT AND FEEL

What emotions flowed out of today's devotional?

How did these emotions guide your experience of the Scripture?

PRAYER

Father,

I am amazed and perplexed that You would allow me to be a temple of your Spirit. You now reside in me permanently, and I am your vessel. You are invited and welcomed here. But I remember, at one point, I was Your enemy. I broke your laws and was in outright rebellion against You. Yet, you choose to walk with me and be my God. Thank you, Father.

Therefore, help me not to adorn Your temple with idols. My flesh still has a craving for physical pleasure. My flesh still has a craving for everything I see. And my flesh still revels in my achievements and possessions. Help me relinquish my fellowship with any darkness so that Your light will shine within me.

In spite of that, You have lavished me with your gifts . . . spiritual gifts that You want me to employ. Help me understand what these gifts are and how I should use them. How might You use them in me today?

DAY 17

Messengers

In the beginning was the Word,
and the Word was with God,
and the Word was God.

John 1:1

And He sent them out to proclaim the kingdom of God.

Luke 9:2

The seventy returned with joy . . .
. . . at that very time He rejoiced greatly in the Holy Spirit.

Luke 10:17 and 10:21

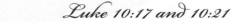

And every day, in the temple and from house
to house, they kept right on teaching and
preaching Jesus as the Christ.

Acts 5:42

The word of God kept on spreading;
and the number of the disciples continued to
increase greatly.

Acts 6:7

So there was much rejoicing in that city.

Acts 8:8

• DAY 17 MUSIC •
https://themessiahadvent.com/day-17/

PREPARE

"The gift of tongues, the beginning of evangelism"

The book of Acts is like an engorged river with water breaking over its banks and rushing everywhere it can settle. The believers proclaim the message that Jesus is the long-awaited Messiah. He was and is the Son of God and wants to redeem His people. This is truth, and it is good news for everybody.

People everywhere received it. Many lives were marked eternally from their activity, including yours. In fact, like a family tree, your faith can be traced back to those very same believers.

READ, LISTEN, HEAR

No 37   Chorus

The Lord gave the word:
great was the company of [the preachers].

Psalm 68:11

No 38   Duet (Soprano, Alto, Chorus)

How beautiful are the feet of them
that preach the gospel of peace,
and bring glad tidings of good things!

Romans 10:15 (Isaiah 52:7)

No 39   Chorus

Their sound is gone out into all lands,
and their words unto the ends of the world.

Romans 10:18 (Psalm 19:4)

REFLECT AND FEEL

What emotions flowed out of today's devotional?

How did these emotions guide your experience of the Scripture?

PRAYER

Father,

This good new of Yours calls me radically in, where I experience a closeness to You that is awesome and overwhelming. But this same message also calls me radically out because this truth is not just for me. Your Messiahship is offered to everyone.

Lord, You have uniquely designed me and placed me here and now. As a result, there are hands that only I can hold. There are ears that will only listen to me.

Give me courage to proclaim the truth about your Kingdom in which I reside. Remind me that when people listen to me, they are really listening to You. And when they reject me, they are really rejecting You.

Remind me that my name is already written in the Book of Life . . . that I have nothing more to accomplish to be accepted. Tell me with whom I should be sharing this good news . . .

DAY 18

Non Serviam

"For long ago I broke your yoke
And tore off your bonds;
But you said, 'I will not serve!'
For on every high hill
And under every green tree
You have lain down as a harlot."

Jeremiah 2:20

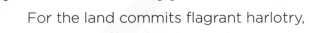

For the land commits flagrant harlotry,
forsaking the Lord.

Hosea 1:2

So when they had finished breakfast,
Jesus said to Simon Peter,
"Simon, son of John, do you love Me more than these?"

John 21:15

• DAY 18 MUSIC •
https://themessiahadvent.com/day-18/

PREPARE

"The world and its ruler reject the Gospel"

The Gospel has reached all four corners of the world, and yet the Prince of Peace does not seem to have delivered.

Where is the peace on earth? Where is the easy yoke?

In the book of Revelation, John refers to "the great harlot." The great harlot seeks to destroy the union of the church's marriage to Christ. The prophets tell us that she had been previously divorced and cast out because of her unfaithfulness. However, she continues to falsely claim to be the "queen" of the spiritual realm.

The "great harlot" has corrupted us to love the world instead of God. Although her claims have seduced us, our fornication with her is consensual.

READ, LISTEN, HEAR

No 40   **Aria (Bass)**

Why do the nations so furiously rage together,
and why do the people imagine a vain thing?
The kings of the earth rise up,
and the rulers take counsel together against the Lord,
and against His anointed.

Psalm 2:1-2 (Acts 4:25-26)

No 41   **Chorus**

Let us break their bonds asunder,
and cast away their yokes from us.

Psalm 2:3

No 42   **Recitative (Tenor)**

He that dwelleth in the heavens shall laugh them to scorn;
the Lord shall have them in derision.

Psalm 2:4

No 43   **Aria (Tenor)**

Thou shalt break them with a rod of iron;
Thou shalt dash them in pieces like a potter's vessel.

Psalm 2:9

REFLECT AND FEEL

What emotions flowed out of today's devotional?

How did these emotions guide your experience of the Scripture?

PRAYER

Father,

Although in some moments I agree with Joshua and say, "As for me and my house, we will serve the Lord," in many others I naturally just go my own way.

Sometimes I find myself just wandering through life, connected to no purpose. I see my to-do list and just put my head down and get busy, not stopping to even consider You or Your plans for me. As much as I don't want to think about it this way, this behavior is rebellion.

However, in other situations, I consciously choose to toss your yoke far from me. I simply have chosen to love this world instead of You, and I go running after what it offers. As much as I don't want to think about it this way, this behavior is adultery . . .

DAY 19

King and Bridegroom

"These will wage war against the Lamb,
and the Lamb will overcome them,
because He is Lord of lords and King of kings,
and those who are with Him
are the called and chosen and faithful."

Revelation 17:14

• DAY 19 MUSIC •

https://themessiahadvent.com/day-19/

PREPARE

"God's triumph"

"The great harlot" has now been judged, and the blood of all her victims has been avenged. Babylon has fallen. We are redeemed.

We only know this because God has supernaturally revealed this to John, the one Jesus loved, and John has written this down for our eyes to see and our hearts to ponder.

Now the Lamb prepares for His rightful marriage to His bride, the church. But before that, we behold His coronation as King.

READ, LISTEN, HEAR

No 44   **Chorus**

Hallelujah!
for the Lord God Omnipotent reigneth.

Revelation 19:6)

The kingdom of this world is become
the kingdom of our Lord,
and of His Christ;
and He shall reign for ever and ever.

Revelation 11:15

KING OF KINGS,
And LORD OF LORDS

Revelation 19:16

REFLECT AND FEEL

What emotions flowed out of today's devotional?

How did these emotions guide your experience of the Scripture?

PRAYER

Father,

As a witness to your crowning as King, I fall to my knees.

You are the Lamb of God, and you suffered and died to take away the sins of the world. You were raised from the dead, and You ascended to heaven.

Now I see that You are rightly the King of all kings and the Lord of all lords. You will reign forever.

I submit myself to you.

Amen

DAY 20

The Beginning of the End

"But after I have been raised,
I will go ahead of you to Galilee."

Matthew 26:32

The angel said to the women,
"Do not be afraid;
for I know that you are looking for Jesus
who has been crucified.
He is not here, for He has risen, just as He said."

Matthew 28:5-6

But the eleven disciples proceeded to Galilee,
to the mountain which Jesus had designated.
When they saw Him, they worshiped Him.

Matthew 28:16-17

For our citizenship is in heaven,
from which also we eagerly wait for a Savior,
the Lord Jesus Christ;
who will transform the body of our humble state
into conformity with the body of His glory,
by the exertion of the power that He has
even to subject all things to Himself.

Philippians 3:20-21

• DAY 20 MUSIC •

https://themessiahadvent.com/day-20/

PREPARE

"The promise of bodily resurrection"

Job was inundated with misfortune related to his entire family, all his belongings, and his personal health. Crushed and beaten down, it would not be a stretch for him to deny the existence of a good God. Job had nothing left to live for, yet he still believed.

After his crucifixion, Jesus showed himself in bodily form for the sake of the disciples but also for you. Jesus' voice resounds more than 2,000 years later: "Blessed *are* they who did not see, and *yet* believed." The victory has been won, and the results are assured.

Our challenge is that we live in the "still to come," a time when we still "fight wars and hear rumors of wars." Take courage! His resurrection reassures us that we can trust the final outcome.

READ, LISTEN, HEAR

No 45   Aria (Soprano)

I know that my redeemer liveth,
and that He shall stand on the latter day upon the earth:
And though worms destroy this body,
yet in my flesh shall I see God.

Job 19:25-26

[For] now is Christ risen from the dead . . .
the firstfruits of them that [sleep].

1 Corinthians 15:20

REFLECT AND FEEL

What emotions flowed out of today's devotional?

How did these emotions guide your experience of the Scripture?

PRAYER

Father,

My eyes have a hard time seeing beyond the material world in front of me—my family and friends, my possessions, and my health. When any of these are disrupted, my whole outlook diminishes. It sends me into a tailspin.

But You returned in bodily form to demonstrate and prove to the disciples and to me that You had overcome our ultimate fear, death. As a result, I no longer need to be afraid of anything. Please help me release the tight grip I have on my material things. Help me see beyond the physical world into the riches of your spiritual kingdom. Set me free into a renewed life.

Father, I do believe. Yet, sometimes I feel the need to place my fingers in Your wounds for reassurance. Help me in my unbelief . . .

DAY 21

Paradox of Life

If we have hoped in Christ in this life only,
we are of all men most to be pitied.

1 Corinthians 15:19

If the dead are not raised,
LET US EAT AND DRINK, FOR TOMORROW WE DIE.

1 Corinthians 15:32

I have been crucified with Christ;
and it is no longer I who live, but Christ lives in me;
and the life which I now live in the flesh
I live by faith in the Son of God,
who loved me and gave Himself up for me.

Galatians 2:20

I came that they may have life, and have it abundantly.

John 10:10

In My Father's house are many dwelling places;
if it were not so, I would have told you;
for I go to prepare a place for you.

John 14:2

• DAY 21 MUSIC •

https://themessiahadvent.com/day-21/

PREPARE

"The promise of redemption from Adam's fall"

If God has power over Jesus' life and death, he also has power over all life and death.

Therefore, we can be comforted that even though these bodies of ours decay and we die, we will also live. Furthermore, we can be encouraged that even though we are still encumbered by our flesh, we will one day receive a renewed body, one that is transformed and imperishable and glorified.

READ, LISTEN, HEAR

No 46   **Chorus**

Since by man came death,
by man came also the resurrection of the dead.
For as in Adam all die,
even so in Christ shall all be made alive.

1 Corinthians 15:21-22

REFLECT AND FEEL

What emotions flowed out of today's devotional?

How did these emotions guide your experience of the Scripture?

PRAYER

Father,

It was important and necessary for You to physically demonstrate that You had power over death because sometimes, Father, I live as if this is it.

Yet, You call me to something more—something beyond what I see.

Make known to me the path of life. Keep reminding me that in Your presence there is fullness of joy; that in Your right hand there are pleasures forever.

May my character and life be marked by an understanding and trust of an abundant and eternal life with You.

Father, I think about others who have gone before me who are dwelling in their prepared places now . . .

DAY 22

Living in the Not Yet

Wretched man that I am!
Who will set me free from the body of this death?
Thanks be to God through Jesus Christ our Lord!

Romans 7:24-25

Then I saw a great white throne and Him who sat
upon it,
from whose presence earth and heaven fled away,
and no place was found for them.
And I saw the dead, the great and the small,
standing before the throne, and books were
opened;
and another book was opened, which is the book
of life;
and the dead were judged from the things
which were written in the books, according to their
deeds.
And the sea gave up the dead which were in it,
and death and Hades gave up the dead which
were in them;
and they were judged, every one of them
according to their deeds.

Revelation 20:11-13

• DAY 22 MUSIC •

https://themessiahadvent.com/day-22/

PREPARE

"The Day of Judgment and general Resurrection"

In spite of our spiritual growth, we still find ourselves doing things that we know we shouldn't. We also don't do the thing that we know we should. The treadmill goes on and on and seems to move faster and faster. Just when we hunker down and get serious about living the Christian life, we find ourselves back at square one. It makes no sense. It seems like for all that God has done for us and if we were truly Christian, that we should buck up and be better by now. How long will this go on?

But on this day, we find that our sinful flesh will finally be released, freeing us to live eternally with Him.

READ, LISTEN, HEAR

No 47   **Recitative (Bass)**

Behold, I tell you a mystery;
We shall not all sleep,
but we shall all be changed
In a moment,
in a twinkling of an eye,
at the last trumpet;

1 Corinthians 15:51-52

No 48   **Aria (Bass)**

the trumpet shall sound,
and the dead shall be raised incorruptible,
and we shall be changed.
For this corruptible must put on incorruption,
and this mortal must put on immortality.

1 Corinthians 15:52-53

REFLECT AND FEEL

What emotions flowed out of today's devotional?

How did these emotions guide your experience of the Scripture?

PRAYER

Father,

It seems sometimes like my effort to be better is in vain. I try and I try and I find myself sinning over and over. My thought life is spoiled. My actions are not consistent with what I say I believe.

Yet, I know now that I will not see full redemption of this worldly flesh until this last trumpet.

How do I deal with this dual nature within me? The endurance required for these trials I experience is overwhelming.

But today, for just a moment, I can see far ahead to the finish line, and it encourages me. Help me place my current trials in perspective. And they are . . .

DAY 23

The Bully Is Neutralized

"I am with you always, even to the end of the age."

Matthew 28:20

Even so consider yourselves to be dead to sin,
but alive to God in Christ Jesus.

Romans 6:11

Therefore, my brethren,
you also were made to die to the Law
through the body of Christ,
so that you might be joined to another,
to Him who was raised from the dead,
in order that we might bear fruit for God.

Romans 7:4

• **DAY 23 MUSIC** •

https://themessiahadvent.com/day-23/

PREPARE

"The victory over death and sin" (Part 1)

Once we grasp that death has been destroyed forever, we are emboldened. We are like a child who has been relentlessly bullied. When we finally trust that a bodyguard has our back, our fear of the bully rescinds and our courage is strengthened to say and do what is right and necessary.

These words from Scripture are included so that we might understand how this plays out for the world and for Satan. It gives us strength in the here and now, in the "not yet time" to release our fear of the bully. Although we still witness the scars of sin, we look beyond to the end and can be encouraged by the outcome.

It is not our strength that has changed our circumstances. It is our trust in Him who loves us and acts on our behalf.

READ, LISTEN, HEAR

No 49   Recitative (Alto)

Then shall be brought to pass the saying that is written,
Death is swallowed up in victory.

1 Corinthians 15:54 (Isaiah 25:8)

No 50   Duet (Alto, Tenor)

O death, where is thy sting?
O grave, where is thy victory?
The sting of death is sin;
and the strength of sin is the law.

1 Corinthians 15:55-56 (Hosea 13:14)

No 51   Chorus

But thanks be to God,
who giveth us the victory
through our Lord Jesus Christ.

1 Corinthians 15:57

REFLECT AND FEEL

What emotions flowed out of today's devotional?

How did these emotions guide your experience of the Scripture?

PRAYER

Father,

As I peer over your broad shoulders at Satan and his schemes, they appear much smaller and insignificant. Sometimes I neglect to remember that You have my back and that You stand with me always.

Lord, throughout my day, when I become disappointed in my lack of righteousness and Satan heckles me with his lies about what a failure I am, remind me again that you have conquered all of this and I can stand strong in You. . .

DAY 24

Costly Grace

But while he was still a long way off,
his father saw him and felt compassion for him,
and ran and embraced him and kissed him.

Luke 15:20

Then he believed in the Lord;
and He reckoned it to him as righteousness.

Genesis 15:6

"And he said to him,
'Son, you have always been with me,
and all that is mine is yours.' "

Luke 15:31

• DAY 24 MUSIC •

https://themessiahadvent.com/day-24/

PREPARE

"The victory over death and sin" (Part 2)

We are full citizens of God's Kingdom. We are legally adopted children of the King. As such, we have received the full inheritance of God. Yet, we did nothing to earn it. It is purely a result of His love for us and His reconciling power with us.

God does all the work. We simply believe in Him.

But the story is not over, is it? We still live in this "not yet" time waiting for the final chapter to unfold. Though Satan and death have been conquered, they still ravage the world. What are we to do? Jesus answers and says to us, "This is the work of God, that you believe in Him whom He has sent."

As we believe in His whole story, we see another way for us today. We begin to follow Him with more and more of our existence. We let go of our longing for this world and what we see. We lean into God and what He would have for us, no matter the cost, because we do not pay a cost. He did. The more we trust Him, the more we realize that we are not obligated to Him, but instead we want Him.

READ, LISTEN, HEAR

No 52   **Aria (Alto)**

If God be for us, who can be against us? . . .
Who shall lay any thing to the charge of God's elect?
It is God that justifieth.
Who is he that condemneth?
It is Christ that died,
yea rather, that is risen again,
who is at the right hand of God,
who makes intercession for us.

Romans 8:31 and 8:33-34

REFLECT AND FEEL

What emotions flowed out of today's devotional?

How did these emotions guide your experience of the Scripture?

PRAYER

Father,

As I understand the whole picture of Your redemption of the world and of me, Your love for me and the extent to which You went to save me overwhelms me.

Father, I believe. Yet, I find my eyes still desiring things of this world. Lord, help me trust You with more of me each day. Peel away the layers of flesh, and reveal the new heart that You have put in me.

Father, as I am reminded of Your forgiveness of me, help me extend kindness and forgiveness to others with ease. Restrain me from counting offenses against others, as You do not count my offenses against You.

Jesus, as I prepare to celebrate Your birth tomorrow, I am going to lay down an area in which I struggle to trust You at the foot of the cross. Intercede on my behalf for the issue of . . .

DAY 25

Benediction

In the beginning was the Word,
and the Word was with God,
and the Word was God.
He was in the beginning with God.
All things came into being through Him,
and apart from Him nothing came into being
that has come into being.
In Him was life, and the life was the Light of men.

John 1:1-4

"I am the Alpha and the Omega,
the first and the last,
the beginning and the end."

Revelation 22:13

For today in the city of David
there has been born for you a Savior,
who is Christ the Lord.

Luke 2:11

"And lo, I am with you always,
even to the end of the age."

Matthew 28:20

• DAY 25 MUSIC •

https://themessiahadvent.com/day-25/

PREPARE

"The glorification of the Messianic victim"

As we come to the end of this Advent devotional, we also find ourselves back at the beginning again as, today, we celebrate Jesus' birth.

Lord Jesus, come.

READ, LISTEN, HEAR

No 53   **Chorus**

Worthy is the Lamb that was slain
and hath redeemed us to God by His blood,
to receive power, and riches, and wisdom,
and strength, and honour,
and glory, and blessing . . .
Blessing, and honour, glory and power, be unto Him
that sitteth upon the throne,
and unto the Lamb
for ever and ever . . .

Amen

Revelation 5:12-13

REFLECT AND FEEL

What emotions flowed out of today's devotional?

How did these emotions guide your experience of the Scripture?

PRAYER

Father God and Lord Jesus,

Direct my way to You. Make me increase and abound in love for all others, as You do for me, so that You may establish my heart as blameless and holy before You, at Your coming, Lord Jesus with all Your saints.

Now to You, to the only God, my Savior, through Jesus Christ my Lord, be glory, majesty, dominion, and authority, before all time and now and forever.

Amen

SMALL GROUP
DISCUSSION GUIDE

The Soul Feels Its Worth can be experienced together as a group. I suggest that each participant experience the daily listening/reading by themselves. Then each week the group can meet for discussions.

WEEK 1: HOPE (DAYS 1-7)

Discussion Questions

Describe your experience of listening to and meditating on Scripture this week.

Was there a moment that was particularly impactful or emotional for you?

Is there an aspect of your life in which you resonate with the feeling of desperation right now?

Is there a promise of God that you cling to when your circumstances go awry?

In what areas of your life do you have the most difficulty trusting God?

WEEK 2: PEACE (DAYS 8-13)

Discussion Questions

Describe your experience of listening to and meditating on Scripture this week.

Was there a moment that was particularly impactful or emotional for you?

God has chosen to make peace with us by His own means. Why do you think God did this?

Even after knowing God's redemptive plan for us, we still find ourselves working to get back into His good graces. Are there areas of your life where you feel that God is disappointed with you? What have you done or will you do in an attempt to "earn" your way back?

How do you respond to being called a sheep?

What circumstances in your life do you blame on God? What do you think this root of bitterness causes you to believe about Him?

How does Jesus' grief speak to you about your value to Him?

WEEK 3: JOY (DAYS 14-19)

Discussion Questions

Describe your experience of listening to and meditating on Scripture this week.

Was there a moment that was particularly impactful or emotional for you?

Is the notion of being subjected to Jesus as a king a positive idea for you or a negative one? Explain.

In what ways do you resist allowing Jesus to be a king over your life?

What ways do you worship the Lord? Being honest, what other things in your life do you also worship?

What are the spiritual gifts that have been lavished upon you?
How do you see them in use (by you)?

Who, in your life, needs to understand the message of Jesus?
How might seeing it as good news change how you might share it?

What do you imagine when you think of the coronation of Christ?
(The Hallelujah chorus)

WEEK 4: LOVE (DAYS 20-25)

Discussion Questions

Describe your experience of listening to and meditating on Scripture this week.

Was there a moment that was particularly impactful or emotional for you?

Are there parts of the Gospel that you have trouble believing or for which you need more proof?

What do you imagine when you think about your own body being resurrected?

How does seeing the finish line help you put your current trials in perspective? What are your current trials?

What lies of Satan do you find yourself dealing with?

What area of your life does Jesus need to intercede in on your behalf?

ACKNOWLEDGMENTS

*T*his book is the result of a long and winding story and there are many characters who have knowingly and unknowingly played a part in its development. As I reflected on this, I wanted to acknowledge some important people who influenced and supported me along the way...

Special thanks are in order for my wife, Karen. She has been a great supporter of all my adventures, hobbies, and meanderings. She was one of the first to try the devotional in its entirety to see if it would fly and she has done a great deal of editing for me. She helps me keep the message clear.

John Lynch's TrueFaced message started me on a journey of beginning to trust Jesus rather than to simply try to please Him. Craig Snyder from Grace Walk Ministries then walked with me, slowly, to understand Grace more fully. This book is ultimately about Grace and I would not have understood the message without their patience and help.

Doug Haupt has been a co-partner in many of my escapades, including this one. We walked into the message of Grace together wobbling and dizzy. He has helped me craft the message within this book and assisted with the filming of the 'making of' video. He helps me not to take myself too seriously.

John Koehler, my publisher and friend, gave me the green light when I first brought the idea about this book to him. His creative brainstorming and boundless creativity make me look better than I deserve.

Daniel Boothe, the Maestro at Symphonicity, was so engaged from the first moment we pitched our crazy idea for Symphonicity to record their live performance of Handel's Messiah. He has opened the floodgates of help and support.

The Sander Center Foundation Giving Circle made a generous grant to Symphonicity enabling them to rent the Sandler Center hall to record Handel's Messiah.

Timo Gomez spent a lot of his time shooting and editing the 'making of' video. His creative eye is amazing and he was a lot of fun to work with.

Calvin Stapert wrote an unbelievable book, Handel's Messiah-Comfort for God's People, which helped me dissect, musically and thematically, what was happening during each movement of Messiah. He translated musical notes and techniques into words and introduced me to concepts like 'Madrigalism' which proved to me that Handel did not do anything accidentally.

Charles Jennens assembled all the Scripture that became the lyrics for Handel's Messiah. Using only words from the Bible, he masterfully told an abridged but complete story of Jesus, the Messiah. His motto for the project was 'Let us sing of greater things'.

George Frideric Handel, the composer of Messiah, captured the story of the Messiah, musically, in a way that makes my hair stand up 300 years after he composed the original music. I can only believe his composition is both genius and inspired. By all standards of music, it should be considered the greatest musical hit of all time.

Lastly, and most importantly, I want to thank Jesus. It is His story that I am re-telling because it is the most important story ever. Jesus demonstrates how much God loves us, and helps us to feel the worth of our souls.